POETRY,
GRIEF,
AND
HEALING

BY
YVONNE REDDICK

Published by
Dog Horn Publishing
45 Monk Ings
Birstall
Batley
WF17 9HU
United Kingdom
doghornpublishing.com

ISBN 978-1-907133-32-9

Typesetting by
Jonathan Penton

Cover design by
Adam Lowe

Sales and distribution by
Inpress Books Ltd.
Milburn House
Dean Street
Newcastle upon Tyne
NE1 1LF
United Kingdom
Telephone: +44 (0) 191 230 8104
Email: orders@inpressbooks.co.uk

CONTENTS

ACKNOWLEDGEMENTS

I am grateful to the following counsellors, who have contributed their wonderful advice to help me create this course: Peter Cardew, Olwen Sutcliffe, Bridget McSweeney, Pat Blackmore.

Thank you also to Adam Lowe, Janusz Jankowski, StJohn Crean, *Magma* poetry magazine, the University of Central Lancashire, and the wonderful poets who have given their permission to have their work included in this booklet.

Writing workshops at the Harris Museum, Gallery and Library, Poetry in Aldeburgh festival, the NHS Lancashire Recovery College and St Catherine's Hospice have been tremendously helpful for allowing me to learn from, and with, people who have been bereaved.

Talking and writing about grief with people at museums and hospices, writing festivals and charities, has taught me so much about loss, losing and beginning to heal.

INTRODUCTION

This booklet is designed to help you write poems in the months and years after bereavement. You don't need to have read or written any poetry before to use it. You can do the writing exercises on your own, or in a group.

It's best to wait until several months after a bereavement before you begin writing. If the loss still feels very raw, you might prefer to wait some time before beginning to write.

This booklet will help you to:

- Read poems about grief, remembering and healing
- Write your own poems, based on easy writing tips
- Use writing to express what you are going through
- Learn how to make a memory box – which can include your poems
- Make a collage of images and write about it
- Imagine taking steps towards healing
- Reflect on what your writing can tell you about yourself

GRIEF: WHY WRITE?

Experiencing the death of a loved one can be deeply painful. It is not always easy to talk to other people about what you are going through.

Writing creates a safe space where you can express your thoughts and feelings, without holding back or being judged. Research has shown that writing to express what you're feeling can help with your wellbeing. You can use writing to get difficult thoughts 'off your chest', and to reflect on your experiences.[1]

These sessions will help you to use poems to explore grief, remembering and healing. You will also have the chance to do

1   See James Pennebaker and Joshya Smyth. *Opening Up by Writing it Down.*

some other creative exercises, such as making a memory box and creating a collage.

SUPPORT DURING BEREAVEMENT

There are details of several organisations that can help you with bereavement and mental health, at the back of this booklet.

WHY POEMS?

Poems can be a great way of expressing what is going on for you.[1] You can write them just for yourself, or you can share them with friends and family. Some people like to read poems at funerals or memorial services. You can also add poems to a memory box: a place to keep things that help you to remember a loved one.

Modern poets such as Denise Riley, Christopher Reid, Pascale Petit and Mona Arshi have all written about their grief at losing loved ones. When you create a poem, you can write it in your own voice, or use the voice of an imaginary character who isn't you. If you are writing about grief and you want to share your poems, you may find this idea helpful, as it means that you don't have to use personal information if you don't want to.

Don't worry too much about the 'quality' of your writing. There's no right or wrong way to write about what's going on for you. The most important thing is to write what you want to write about, be creative and express yourself.

1   For information about poetry therapy, see Nicholas Mazza. *Poetry Therapy: Theory and Practice.* Abingdon: Routledge, 2016.

If you love prose or stories, it's fine to write things out that way if you like. You can always add in some line breaks afterwards to shape your poem. Or if you prefer, you can write a prose poem! There are examples of prose poems by Malika Booker and Kathleen Jamie in this booklet.

If you find this booklet helpful, please get in touch! I would be happy to hear from you: yreddick@uclan.ac.uk.

WRITING FOR WELLBEING

SESSION 1: THE ART OF LOSING

We will begin to think about loss and explore the feelings that come of it. We will look at poems about losing something or someone very precious, and write our own.

The writing prompts will show you how to write a list-poem, based some examples, and consider the process of making a memory box.

Beginning: Losing an Object

- Think of an object that you've lost.
- What were your thoughts, feelings and behaviour when you lost it?

QUICK WRITING EXERCISE

Think about a time when you have lost something, e.g. keys, glasses, jewellery. Note down:

1. The first thing you did
2. The second thing you did
3. What you thought
4. What you felt
5. What happened afterwards

You can use these notes to help you begin to draft a poem later.

THE ART OF LOSING

What you might notice is that all kinds of emotions come up when you lose something useful. If someone loses their glasses, they may:

- refuse to believe that they've actually lost them, and look in the same place several times
- feel angry with themselves for not remembering where the glasses are
- feel sad that the glasses really are lost
- feel anxious about how they will see
- finally accept that the glasses aren't going to turn up again.

These emotions are similar to the ones we feel when a person we love has died, although when we are bereaved, they are far more intense. Thinking about how we feel when we lose an object is useful for showing us how many different feelings may come up.

Counsellors and therapists used to think that we go through different 'stages' of grief: denial, anger, bargaining, depression and acceptance. While this idea is not current any more, we definitely go through a huge range of emotions – sometimes several different ones at the same time.

Here are some poems about losing something – or someone – really precious. What do they make you think about when you read them?

Malika Booker's aunt loses (then finds) something she really treasures.

from FAITH

That day you lost your rosary for two days,
we search under beds and in fruit bowls.
You cry nonstop all night. Nurses sift mountains
of soiled sheets until the rosary is found nestled
in your dirty pillow case. When they give it to you,
your fingers continue rolling as if it had not strayed.

Malika Booker. *Pepper Seed*. Leeds: Peepal Tree, 2013.

Mona Arshi remembers the moment when someone phoned her when she was on a train, to tell her that her brother had died.

from PHONE CALL ON A TRAIN JOURNEY

Something's lost, she craves it
hunting in pockets, sleeves,

checks the eyelets in fabric.
Could you confirm you were his sister?

Mona Arshi. *Small Hands*. Liverpool: Pavilion, 2015.

Elizabeth Bishop writes about the things that she has lost, and thinks about the end of a relationship. This poem is also useful for thinking about the process of grieving. You can look at her poem 'One Art' online, on the Poetry Foundation website::

Lists of objects are a helpful way to start poems. Here are some poems whose authors think about the person they have lost, and list objects associated with them.

Karen McCarthy Woolf remembers her baby son Otto, by creating a list of objects associated with him.

WHITE BUTTERFLIES

Three white butterflies
flutter then land
on the artichoke spikes
in the walled garden.

White sky against the ash.
The wind in the leaves
a rush of sighs.

White lavender
at the edge of the pool.
White hydrangeas
wilted in the bouquet.
White lilies sticky with scent.
White tissues in the box.
White linen on the bed.
White curtains shrunk in the wash.
White muslin squares.

Your tiny white vests, unworn.

Karen McCarthy Woolf. *An Aviary of Small Birds*. Manchester: Carcanet, 2014.

Writing Exercise: Things We'll Keep

- Write down some of the things that you'll keep to remind you of the person you've lost. Write down why you're going to keep them.
- Write down up to 5 objects and reasons.

These objects and reasons will help us to write a list-poem later. These are also objects that you could use to create a memory box after these writing exercises.

Example Poem

Mona Arshi remembers her brother by listing some of the objects that she receives after his death.

Phone Call on a Train Journey

The smallest bone in the human ear
weighs no more than a grain of rice.

She keeps thinking it means something
but probably is nothing.

Something's lost, she craves it
hunting in pockets, sleeves,

checks the eyelets in fabric.
Could you confirm you were his sister?

When they pass her his rimless glasses,
they're tucked into a padded sleeve;

several signatures later,
his rucksack is in her hands

(without the perishables),
lighter than she had imagined.

Mona Arshi. *Small Hands*. Liverpool: Pavilion, 2015.

In this poem, Yvonne Reddick remembers her dad and names some of the mountains where she went hiking with him. She lists the objects she received after his sudden death in the hills.

RISK

The way he carried two compasses
in case one failed,
spare batteries for the GPS,

and jotted each leg of the journey
on an envelope, in a left-handed scrawl
no-one else could decipher.

The way he turned back
from the plateau of Wyvis
as clouds were glooming

and my friend's pack was a dead weight
of hairbrushes and spare socks;
tackled the Buachaille and the Ben

by the least craggy routes,
shunned cliffs, snow cornices.
(I was the one who tobogganed

down June snowfields, whooping.)
He rushed to save his camera first
when he fell chest-deep

into a stinking peat-bog,
and hoarded all his Ordnance Surveys
going back to 1976.

The way what came back
was a map, still legible
despite the bleeding ink.

A sealed survival bag.
His damp wool hat and gloves.

Yvonne Reddick. *Translating Mountains*. Bridgford: Seren, 2017.

WRITING EXERCISE: A LIST-POEM

1. Look back at your lists of objects and feelings/associations. Look back at the example poems for inspiration.

2. Write a poem about:

- Some of the things you're going to keep, and feelings/ memories/ reasons associated with those objects

Write one line for every object, or more if you'd like to.

Making a Memory Box

When a loved one has passed away, some people worry that they are going to forget them. Although this doesn't usually happen, you might find it helpful to record memories and keep mementos of your loved one.

You can look at the objects in the memory box whenever you want, to remind you that your special person still plays a part in your life, even though they are gone. Here's how to make one.

1. Find a box big enough to take the things that you would like to keep. A shoebox is ideal. You can decorate it if you like.

2. Now, it's time to fill it! Here are some of the things that you might like to include:

- Photos
- CDs of music
- Cards or letters that you have written to your loved one
- Keepsakes from trips, such as holiday or cinema tickets
- Favourite pieces of clothing or jewellery
- Poems you have written using this leaflet

Some of the memories may make you smile; others may make you feel sad. It is perfectly normal to feel upset when you are grieving, and this is nothing to be ashamed of.

You can also look at this leaflet from Havens Hospice for more information: tinyurl.com/havenshospice.

SELF-CARE

What do you do to take care of yourself? Write down a few examples, e.g.:

- Making yourself a cup of tea
- Spending time with a friend
- Getting some fresh air
- Doing some exercise
- Enjoying a favourite hobby

What can you do to take care of yourself after this session?

SESSION 2:
RIVERS AND WATERFALLS

'If life is a river and your heart is a boat …'
The Corrs – 'Heaven Knows (No Frontiers)'

We will spend this session looking at images to describe life's
ups and downs.

If life can be seen as a river, bereavement can be viewed
as going over a waterfall. We can experience a whirlpool of
different emotions. We will look at different metaphors for
grief. We will read poems in different forms and styles, and
write our own.

'LIFE IS A RIVER'

1. We are going to think about images that can help us to consider life's ups and downs.

If we think of life as a river, we can think of bereavement as like a waterfall.

'If life is a river and your heart is a boat' – The Corrs

These are two **metaphors**: describing a thing as representing something else.

'Live like a mighty river' – Ted Hughes, letter to his son Nicholas.

In poetic terms, this is a **simile** – a thing described as **like** something else.

2. Make some of your own metaphors. Use these prompts if you would like:

Today, my mind is …
This morning has been a …
I want tomorrow to be …

3. Put some of your metaphors together to create a short poem.

If you like, you can try the form of a **haiku.**

The Poetry Foundation calls this 'a Japanese verse form most often composed, in English versions, of three unrhymed lines of five, seven, and five syllables. A haiku often features an image, or a pair of images, meant to depict the essence of a specific moment in time.'

Example Poems: Watery Haikus

Frog

Winter's pond, ancient –
frog emerges, leaps, striking
water's percussion.

Basho, translated by Adam Lowe.

594

River bed rising
Underwater, feet downstream
The rock tops are slick

806

Sky colored skyline
Skyscraper glass river blue
Boats with no covers

975

Water skippers flick
Tiny ripples on the bend
Each interrupted

Calvin Olsen. From *Ten Thousand Haiku: 27 years of 17 syllable days*.
tenthousandhaiku.com/tag/river

METAPHOR AND THE POETS

'Grief is the thing with feathers' – Max Porter
'Grief is a Mouse' – Emily Dickinson
'Grief thief of time' – Dylan Thomas
Grief is paper on the floor, a shoehorn, a laundry ticket and cigarette smoke in Charles Bukowski's 'Consummation of Grief'.

QUICK WRITING EXERCISE

Make up some of your own metaphors, beginning, 'Grief is …'

Here are two poems that treat grief differently. They are written in different styles and they form different shapes on the page. Which one do you prefer?

Maria Isakova Bennett remembers a family friend, using images of colour and trees to think about peace at the end of life.

PRAYER FOR DANIEL

for lapis when I wake
for backdrop
perfect contrast to chlorophyll made shy

for November-blue   for
the birch tree   its shedding
                        leaving space for
space for   space to reach for

for cold nights and short days
for sugar   sweet sugar   trapped
and making anthocyanins
turning birch tops
            into crowns of gold

for the purity of blue   for its grace
for branches like golden anthers
for radiance   for soul

for day three of Daniel's last days
    nature's course they call it
consultants
    oncologists   and nurses

34

for day three of his
three hundred and sixty-five
for each day
for each of us
For Daniel's days   all gone

Maria Isakova Bennett

Jamaican poet Delroy McGregor remembers his Uncle Garry.
He uses some dialect words that he and his Uncle Garry would
use.

UNCLE GARRY

Me memba yuh ganja smoke,
yuh dreadlocks, di way yuh
cuss yuh claat, yuh old shoes,
yuh yellow mesh marina. Me
memba di machete yuh used
to cut di yard, di jelly, di cane,
di coconut. Me memba di way
yuh mad when yuh short a spliff,
di fry dumpling an chicken late
a night, di smell a seasoning.
Me memba how yuh scale
di fish in a di yard, di night
dem we spen pon di roof a talk
bout family, a talk bout life,
a talk bout people weh love talk
bout people. Me memba di day
yuh cut yuh locks. Yuh smoke
yuh weed yes, tell yuh story
dem yes, cut di cane yes,
but someting neva right. More
while yuh gone in a di night,
an nuh come back till a morning,
yuh stop di reasoning, yuh stop

di seasoning, yuh stop fry dumplin,
yuh staat go road wid di bad people
dem. Me neva bawl when me hear
seh dem chop yuh up, me neva come
a yuh funeral, me stop talk bout yuh,
cuz me staat teck yuh advice.

Delroy McGregor, *Magma* 75: Loss (Winter 2019).

WRITING PROMPT

Write your own image for grief, beginning: 'Grief is...'

Use your image as a starting point for your own poem.

- Like Delroy McGregor, you can use strong rhythms and repetition to make your poem flow.
- Or, like Maria Isakova Bennett, you can use gaps and silences to create space in your poem.

A Final Thought

Ted Hughes thinks about life and survival in terms of a great river.

from The River

Fallen from heaven, lies across
The lap of his mother, broken by world.

But water will go on
Issuing from heaven

In dumbness uttering spirit brightness ...

Ted Hughes. *Collected Poems*. London: Faber & Faber, 2003.

SELF-CARE

What are you planning to do to take care of yourself after this session?

SESSION 3: REMEMBERING

In this session, we will think about the process of remembering a room in a house where we used to live. We will read some poems that remember a place or person, and try writing our own. We will think about which styles of poetry we prefer.

We will also look at collaging to capture memories and express states of mind, and try writing in response to a collage.

Visualisation exercise

1. Imagine a room in a house where you used to live.

- Walk through it in your mind's eye.
- What does it look like?
- What can you hear?
- Who else is there?

2. We are going to write about a home we used to live in, and what it causes us to remember.

Think about what you saw, in your mind's eye, during the visualisation exercise.

Jot down:

- Three objects you saw
- What the house smells like
- What you imagine hearing when walking through it
- The people you think of when you walk through the house
- What you see them doing, in your mind's eye

Revisiting somewhere where we used to live can help us to think about how we remember our past, and how it connects to where we are now.

Here are some poems about remembering.

- Do they bring back any memories or associations for you?
- Is there a particular style of poem here that you prefer?

from NINE NIGHTS

SONG

Grief song is a different story. A clap of hands then
a rocking back and forth story. Grief song is a body
dancing to a jagged melody story. Grief song is so
searing, it's the belly drops to knees story. Grief song is
the way his mother sinks into the arms of *Rock of Ages*
story. I tell you Grief song is a hard to tell story.

Malika Booker. *Poetry Review*, Autumn 2016.

Our father

Our father in blackberries just beyond reach
of my bramble-torn fingers

Our father in the fierce bed of nettle
along the dim gully

Our father in the flesh of a plum where the wasp
has bored to the stone

Our father in chickens squawking for nothing
in the dark barn

Our father in the orchard whose juiciest windfalls
I'm gorging on

Our father in the shed with the axe and the dried
tin of creosote

Our father in the milky stems of figs pulled
too soon from the tree

Our father in snow that hardens and melts
round my boots

Our father in the green and rain all round
the dark cottage

Our father in the smell of your books and the trunk
they returned them in

Sarah Wedderburn. *Magma* 75: Loss (Winter 2019).

BONE RAILROAD

I will clutch your bones together
into a coral palace at the bottom
of the sea. I will sing hymns

to celebrate you in the vault
built from your ribcage. The stained
glass I will blow from your dreams.

Who cast you down here like
a bone railroad from Africa's west
coast to the Americas, the Caribbean?

Whales will worship you.
I will come down and sit upon
your coral throne, and remember

who you were. I will unearth
your stories, find the ships that
discarded you, and sink them all.

Adam Lowe. *Precocious*. Birstall: Fruit Bruise Press, 2012.

Writing Ideas: A Memory Poem

Use one of these prompts if you want to – or you are welcome to follow your own ideas.

1. Like Malika Booker, write about funeral songs, customs and rituals.

OR

2. Like Sarah Wedderburn, write about objects, buildings and places that hold memories for you.

OR

3. Like Adam Lowe, unearth a story about an issue that is important to you.

COLLAGING MEMORIES

Find some old newspapers and magazines. Pick out some images and words that appeal to you.

Make a collage out of them. Use them to express some of these ideas:

1. What do you want to remember?

OR

2. What do you want to 'get off your chest'?

Try writing a short poem – 5-8 lines – using some of the words and images from your collage. If you like, you can write about yourself from the perspective of another person. For example:

'She wants to remember the house …'
'He wants to talk about the empty chair …'

Self-care

What are you going to do to take care of yourself after this session?

A Final Thought

Here's a poem about how grief is a shared experience across cultures, but also how it can bring unexpected possibilities.

Reflections at a Tibetan Buddhist Monastery in Dharamshala, India

A man sweeps the middle of a courtyard
The monastery is a pregnant woman, swelling with seekers –
That old woman, her fingers moving a worn rosary
The soft hill of her back rising, falling with every breath,
Smiling a toothless smile, sharing sweets with a friend

A young Buddhist monk walks a corridor dotted with yellow doors
Robes a river of wine, his face is moonlight
The low chanting of Tibetan monks is warm oil on a dry body

And everywhere, they sit with rosaries
That one – grief, a heavy sack of grain on his chest
That one – suckling an infant, her body moving to the chants
And of course, that one – the ageing, white spiritual aspirant,
her wrists ringed with amethyst and silver

In the monastery, we are all equalised –
the man with the broken spirit on the corner
mingles with the blithe toddler skipping on the steps
Karma is always the young boy putting on his red
canvas sneakers to play hide and seek

The sweeping ends, the chanting stops
Everyday sounds fill the monastery –
the ring of a cellphone, the laughter of friends

All around us, in the dead leaves being swept up,
in the people spinning the prayer wheel,
in the young girl eating a biscuit,
in the rush of people leaving to start their days,
loss is a door opening to fresh possibilities

Jhilmil Breckenridge. *Magma* 75: Loss (Winter 2019).

SESSION 4:
THE MASKS WE WEAR

In this session, we will use masks to think about the inner and outer 'layers' of ourselves, and what we reveal to other people. We will then try writing about the masks we wear!

MASKS

Masks are a useful way of thinking about how we show ourselves to other people. We reveal different aspects of ourselves to different people, depending on the situation.

WE WEAR THE MASK
Paul Laurence Dunbar (1872-1906)

We wear the mask that grins and lies,
It hides our cheeks and shades our eyes,—
This debt we pay to human guile;
With torn and bleeding hearts we smile,
And mouth with myriad subtleties.

Why should the world be over-wise,
In counting all our tears and sighs?
Nay, let them only see us, while
    We wear the mask.

We smile, but, O great Christ, our cries
To thee from tortured souls arise.
We sing, but oh the clay is vile
Beneath our feet, and long the mile;
But let the world dream otherwise,
    We wear the mask!

- What does it make you think about?
- Does it describe any situations you've been in?

Things to think about:

- We may show different 'layers' of ourselves at different points when we are bereaved. For example, we may feel that we have to show the calm 'outer' layer in public, but we may want to show people close to us an 'inner' layer that is upset.
- We may wish that we could show more people what our inner self is thinking.

TAKE A LOOK AT THESE POEMS

Do they bring back any memories or associations for you?

Adam Lowe takes inspiration from the myth of Narcissus – who fell
in love with his own reflection!

NARCISSUS

This is the closest I have come
to feeling submerged. My crown
glitters wetly in the bathe of sunlight.
Koi fish suck kisses at my neck,
at the nook of my arms, behind
my knees, at the blue stems where
my blood whispers your name
in ultrasound. The deep music
of ocean, the company of algae,
cannot cover the chorus of need
that swishes and thrashes and bleeds.
I stare out, through the surface
of the water, to see if you see me
here amongst the reeds. You smile,
but only to admire your reflection.

Adam Lowe. *Precocious*. Birstall: Fruit Bruise Press, 2012.

In the next poem, on the opposite page, Adam Lowe re-imagines the
Biblical queen, Jezebel.

Jezebel, Guilty, Queen

You call me Jezebel: temptress of men, seducer in the garden, false idol
in the spotlight of false gods, pedlar of blasphemy and unnatural sex.

You call me guilty: unsuitable for marriage, shock slut of back alleys,
brazen siren on land, seed-spilling succubus who visits in the night.

You call me a queen, as in my cell I paint myself Anne Boleyn,
like so many headless queens before me. Paste on my make-up, set
    myself

sharp and glittery in jewels, clutch at pearls as sexy rosaries,
and know, when you silence me, at least I'll go down in history.

Adam Lowe. *Filigree: Contemporary Black British Poetry*. Leeds: Peepal Tree Press, 2019.

TAKE A LOOK AT SOME OF THESE IMAGES.

Which one appeals to you most?
What do they make you think of?

ID 85917755 © Kiosea39 | Dreamstime.com

WRITE A POEM ABOUT YOUR MASK

Some of these ideas might help you to get started:

- What does your mask look like? (It can be a real facial expression, or an imagined theatre mask/disguise).
- Is there anything you wish you could show to the outside world?

Collaging Ideas

Find some old newspapers and magazines. Pick out some images and words that appeal to you.

Make a collage out of them. Use them to express some of these ideas:

3. Which images/words make you think about your mask?

OR

4. Which images/words represent the 'real' self behind the mask?

If you are writing in a group, you might like to share some thoughts about your collage.

A Final Thought

All

Just before dawn
you are in a bright field, a ploughed
and stubbled, slowly sloping field
in late afternoon, in autumn, in England.

You are lying in that field
and two owls are cradling you.
You have lain down, at the edge
of a town, and they have come.

You were worried, as if wounded,
that you would never get up again
in time; that something had been buried
and would stay hidden forever;

that the leaves would fall from those oak trees
and would be the last leaves (they are falling now);
or that you would slip back, happy and lost,
into your childhood.

And they comfort you, these two companions,
their tawny, otherly wings, as you sleep there
on the dark ploughed earth
at the edge of that town,

caressing your face
like a mother's touch,
and telling you,

these low owls,
these slow owls,
that all is well.

And that is all:
and that is all.

Robert Powell. *All*. Scarborough: Valley Press, 2015.

If writing about loss has stirred up some difficult emotions, you might find that an uplifting poem like this one is helpful.

Self-care

What are you going to do to take care of yourself after this session?

SESSION 5:
IMAGINING HEALING

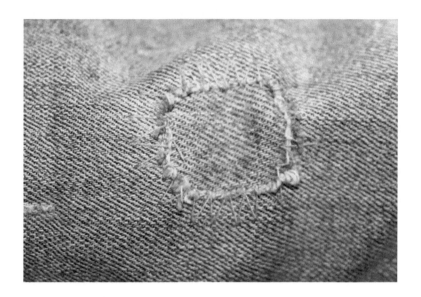

Image by _Alicja_ from Pixabay

If you have just lost a loved one, healing may seem a long way away. Grieving can take many months or years, and there is no fixed timeframe for it. It's OK to feel sad for as long as is right for you.

This session will help us to imagine healing visualise a healing place or imagine caring for the self. We will also look at the ways we can take care of ourselves at a difficult time.

HEALINGS 1
KATHLEEN JAMIE

Sometimes I almost hear a sweet wild music a kind of fairy music at the edge of sense. It's audible in the spaces between the rowan leaves, in the breeze, in the robin's song, in the sound of the distant traffic whose destination is nothing to do with me.

The sound of a handing over, the best surrender. The sound of knots untying themselves, the sound of the benign indifference of the world.

Kathleen Jamie and Brigid Collins. *Frissure*. Edinburgh: Polygon, 2013.

Frissure is a book by poet Kathleen Jamie and artist Brigid Collins. *Frissure* was inspired by Kathleen Jamie's experiences of surgery for breast cancer, which left her with a scar. Brigid Collins drew the shape of the scar and used its form to create natural images. Kathleen Jamie wrote prose-poems about the process of healing.

In this session, we will explore how to heal the inner self, rather than the physical body.

OPENING EXERCISE: GUIDED VISUALISATION

We will think about where we are now and imagine a place where we can find healing.

1. Make sure you're sitting comfortably in a quiet place.
2. Imagine a place where your healing is. It could be a room in a house, or a peaceful place outdoors.
3. Begin to explore the place where your healing is. Spend some time there.
4. What do you see? What do you hear?
5. Remember that if you are going through a tough time, you can imagine going to the place where your healing is.

Note down where your healing place is, so that you'll know where you can find it if you need it.

Here are some poems that visit healing places, in times of stress or grief. Do you have a favourite?

THE LAKE ISLE OF INNISFREE

I will arise and go now, and go to Innisfree,
And a small cabin build there, of clay and wattles made:
Nine bean-rows will I have there, a hive for the honey-bee;
And live alone in the bee-loud glade.

And I shall have some peace there, for peace comes
    dropping slow,
Dropping from the veils of the morning to where the
    cricket sings;
There midnight's all a glimmer, and noon a purple glow,
And evening full of the linnet's wings.

I will arise and go now, for always night and day
I hear lake water lapping with low sounds by the shore;
While I stand on the roadway, or on the pavements grey,
I hear it in the deep heart's core.

W. B. Yeats

Karen McCarthy Woolf remembers her baby son Otto, and imagines his spirit. (The 'octobrine' is an imaginary bird invented by the poet Pablo Neruda.)

AN AVIARY OF SMALL BIRDS

My love is an aviary
of small birds
and I must learn
to leave the door ajar…

Are you the sparrow
who landed when I sat
at a slate table
sowing lettuces?

Webbs Wonder, Lollo
Rosso, English Cos…
Swift and deft
you flit and peck peck

quick as the light that
constitutes your spirit.
Yes, you were briefer
than Neruda's octobrine.

So much rain that night.
Our room is an ocean
where swallows dive.
The bubble bursts

too soon, too late, too long:
all sorts of microscopia
swim upstream, float in
on summer's storm.

The tenor of your heart
is true as a tuning fork struck
—and high! My love
is the bird who flies free.

Karen McCarthy Woolf. *An Aviary of Small Birds*. Manchester: Carcanet, 2015.

Take a look at Louis Hoffman's article 'Can a Poem Be Healing? Writing Poetry Through the Pain': tinyurl.com/healingpoetry.

HEALING POEMS

Try writing your own poem about healing. Pick one of the following prompts if you need something to start you off.

- Write a poem set in a place where you can find healing.
- Begin with 'My love is ...'

SELF-CARE

What are you going to do after this session to take care of
yourself?

SESSION 6: REFLECTING ON WHERE WE ARE AND LEARNING FROM OUR POEMS

This session is all about considering where we are now, in terms of what's going on for us. We will think about the way grief is not a straightforward journey, and how we may find ourselves going sideways or even backwards.

We will use our poems to learn more about ourselves. The 'quality' of the poems doesn't matter. What is important is what they reveal about us. There are also some ideas for sharing your poems with someone else, if that's something you'd like to do. There is also a list of poetry books for different kinds of grief, which you might like to read.

INTRODUCTORY EXERCISE

We will think about how we have experienced the process of grieving. Things may change from when the grief is at its most intense, to a few weeks, months or years after the event.

We can even score our feelings on a scale of 1 to 10 (1 = feeling awful, 10 = feeling great.) If it is helpful, we can use colours to imagine our state of mind (black = feeling upset; green = feeling peaceful.)

WHERE I WAS

Be aware of what it was like when the grief was most intense. You don't have to relive those emotions, but just notice what they were like.
- What words spring to mind?
- How were you interacting with other people?
- Do you associate any colours with that time?
- Could you score your emotions on a scale from 1 to 10?

WHERE I AM NOW

- What words spring to mind?
- How are you interacting with other people?

- Do you associate any colours with where you are now?
- Could you score your emotions on a scale from 1 to 10?

Have you noticed any change between where you were when the grief was intense, and where you are now?

Grief isn't always a forward journey: sometimes we are shifted backwards or even sideways.

Pathway Poetry

Poet Fawzia Kane, from Trinidad and Tobago, remembers a loved one who made a crossing.

Limbo

Sea mist has rolled in too quick tonight. He must
be there, on the other side, where the bridge meets
land. Perhaps it's hiding his shape. I remember

that hot day here, so many years ago, he stood
under sea-almond trees, chatting to fisherfolk
while they tended their seine. He'd stopped the car

for me to walk back along the unsteady boards,
to film the stretch and curve of suspended cables,
how their vertical strands swung in slight breezes

yet kept their strength, held tight over the lagoon.
The water was a clearer blue then, deeper than
that day's sky even, beyond the black mangrove

that wrapped around the river's mouth. Pirogues
had moored along the banks, their sides clanked
with red/white/black stripes, names of *Paradiso*

and *La Divina* painted on in untidy letters. Now,
all that remains for us, years later, is that path
across a swaying bridge, lined with wooden boards.

The shadows cause its rough grain to sharpen, make
the boards into lines that seem to move and spool
out as we walk, always tracking ahead of our steps.

Fawzia Kane. *Magma* 75: Loss (Winter 2019).

WRITING EXERCISE: RIVERS AND PATHS

Here are some images of waterways and pathways. Pick one that appeals to you.

Pathways and Waterways Poem

Think about where you were, and where you would like to be. Use the picture you have chosen as a starting point if you want.

Note down a few words in answer to these questions:

- What did the view look like when your grief was at its most intense? (Weather, landscape, terrain, scenery…?)
- What does the view look like now?
- Are there any times where you have gone backwards or sideways?
- What does the view look like where you'd like to be in the future?

Now turn your notes into a poem about the 'journey' of grief. You might like to use a regular form and rhymes. If you prefer, you can give your poem a freer form.

What We Can Learn From Our Own Poems

Take another look at a poem that you have written during these writing sessions.

We have seen how poems can help us to express powerful emotions, but also how they can prompt us to think about those emotions.

Reread your poem to yourself. Think about:

- What are you expressing in the poem?
- What does it mean to you?
- What can it tell you about yourself?
- Does it help you to visualise any new ideas about your situation, e.g. how you would like things to be?

If you like, you can share your poem with someone else, and they can tell you what they think it says about your experiences.

Things to talk about when sharing poems:

- What does it tell you about the other person?
- Are there any experiences in the poem that you have gone through too?

Poetry 'Prescriptions' for Further Reading

Poems about Bereavement

Adam Lowe and Yvonne Reddick, eds. *Magma* 75: Loss.
Kevin Young, ed. *The Art of Losing: Poems of Grief and Healing*.
New York: Bloomsbury, 2010.

Life-Affirming Poems

Deborah Alma, ed. *The Emergency Poet: An Anti-Stress Poetry Anthology*. London: Michael O'Mara, 2015.
Neil Astley, ed. *Staying Alive: Real Poems for Unreal Times*. Tarset: Bloodaxe, 2002.
Robert Powell. *All*. Scarborough: Valley Press, 2015.

Grieving for a Husband, Wife or Partner

Mark Doty. *Atlantis*. London: Jonathan Cape, 1995.
Deryn Rees-Jones. *Burying the Wren*. Bridgford: Seren, 2012.
----. *And You, Helen*. Bridgford: Seren, 2014.
Christopher Reid. *A Scattering*. Oxford: Arete, 2009.

Grieving for a Child

Rebecca Goss. *Her Birth*. Manchester: Carcanet, 2013.
Karen McCarthy Woolf. *An Aviary of Small Birds*. Manchester: Carcanet, 2014.
Denise Riley. *Say Something Back*. London: Picador, 2016.

Grieving for a Sibling

Mona Arshi. *Small Hands*. Liverpool: Pavilion, 2015.
Matthew and Michael Dickman. *Brother*. London: Faber & Faber, 2016.

Grieving for a Friend

Alice Kinsella. *Flower Press*. Oxford: The Onslaught Press, 2018.
Don Paterson. *Rain*. London: Faber & Faber, 2009.

Grieving for a Parent

Emily Berry. *Stranger, Baby*. London: Faber & Faber, 2017.
Elizabeth Burns. *The Shortest Days*. Stromness: Galdragon, 2008.
Kayo Chingonyi. *Kumukanda*. London: Chatto, 2017.
John Fennelly. *Another Hunger*. Sheffield: smith/doorstop, 2018.
Ann Gray. *I Wish I Had More Mothers*. Sheffield: smith/doorstop, 2018.
Philip Gross. *Later*. Tarset: Bloodaxe, 2013.
Mimi Khalvati. *Earthshine*. Sheffield: smith/doorstop, 2013.
Andrew Motion. *The Cinder Path*. London: Faber & Faber, 2009.

Grieving for a Difficult Relative:

Paul Deaton. *A Watchful Astronomy*. Bridgford: Seren, 2017.
David Morley. *The Magic of What's There*. Manchester: Carcanet, 2017.
Pascale Petit. *Mama Amazonica*. Tarset: Bloodaxe, 2017.
----. *Fauverie*. Bridgford: Seren, 2013.

Traumatic Bereavement:

Nick Flynn. *Some Ether*. Minneapolis: Graywolf, 2000.
Yvonne Reddick. *Translating Mountains*. Bridgford: Seren, 2017.

WAR, RACIST PERSECUTION, RELIGIOUS PERSECUTION

Seamus Heaney. *North*. London: Faber & Faber, 1975.
Nick Makoha. *Kingdom of Gravity*. Leeds: Peepal Tree, 2017.
Claudia Rankine. *Citizen: An American Lyric*. London: Penguin, 2015.
Ocean Vuong. *Night Sky with Exit Wounds*. London: Cape, 2016.

EXPERIENCING TERMINAL ILLNESS

Elizabeth Burns. *Lightkeepers*. Lancaster: Wayleave, 2016.
Helen Dunmore. *Inside the Wave*. Tarset: Bloodaxe, 2017.

SUPPORT DURING BEREAVEMENT

CRUSE BEREAVEMENT CARE

The Cruse Bereavement Care Freephone National Helpline is staffed by trained bereavement volunteers, who offer emotional support to anyone affected by bereavement. The number is **0808 808 1677**. You can also email: **helpline@cruse.org.uk**. *cruse.org.uk/get-help*

DYING MATTERS

Dying Matters has many resources to help with the process of grieving. *dyingmatters.org/page/coping-bereavement*

Mental Health Support

You can call NHS 111 if you have a mental health condition that becomes worse, but is not life threatening.

Samaritans have a free service to call 24 hours a day, 365 days a year, if you want to talk to someone confidentially about your mental health. Call them on 116123.

Counsellors

British Association for Counselling & Psychotherapy (BACP)-accredited counsellors in your area.
counselling-directory.org.uk/bacpcharity.html

ND - #0189 - 270225 - C43 - 229/152/5 - PB - 9781907133329 - Gloss Lamination